What in the World Is That?

World Is

That?

By Margie O'Hern

Scott Foresman
is an imprint of

Glenview, Illinois • Boston, Massachusetts • Chandler, Arizona •
Upper Saddle River, New Jersey

Illustrations
6, 9 Jeff Grunewald.

Photographs

Every effort has been made to secure permission and provide appropriate credit for photographic material. The publisher deeply regrets any omission and pledges to correct errors called to its attention in subsequent editions.

Unless otherwise acknowledged, all photographs are the property of Pearson Education, Inc.

Photo locators denoted as follows: Top (T), Center (C), Bottom (B), Left (L), Right (R), Background (Bkgd)

Opener Eric Rorer/Aurora/Getty Images; **1** ©Dennis Flaherty/Getty Images; **4** World Picture Network; **5** Brian Cosgrove/©DK Images; **7** ©Terry Sirrell/Getty Images; **8** R H Productions/Corbis; **10** ©Phototake, Inc/Alamy Images; **11** Gregg Newton/SouthernCross Images/Corbis; **12** Gregg Newton/Corbis; **13** ©Alan Highton; **14** ©Alan Highton; **15** Peter Arnold, Inc.; **16** United States Department of the Interior; **17** ©Dennis Flaherty/Getty Images; **18** Felix Stensson/Alamy Images; **19** Map Resources; **20** Javier Trueba/MSF/Photo Researchers, Inc..

ISBN 13: 978-0-328-51659-9
ISBN 10: 0-328-51659-7

TABLE OF CONTENTS

Chapter 1

Is That a Fire Rainbow?

What has the colors of a rainbow but isn't really a rainbow? It's a **fire rainbow**—a halo of color caused by sunlight shining through ice crystals in cirrus clouds. The scientific name for this is a circumhorizontal arc. It often looks like a halo completely encircling the sun, and at other times it looks like an inverted rainbow.

When people first saw this **phenomenon**, or remarkable event, they thought it looked as if the clouds were on fire. They also saw the same colors we see in a rainbow, so they called it a fire rainbow.

A fire rainbow in Coeur d'Alene, Idaho, in June 2006

Cirrus clouds form high in the atmosphere, higher than 20,000 feet.

A fire rainbow occurs only in cirrus clouds, which contain wispy strands of ice **crystals**. Cirrus clouds form at upper levels of the atmosphere. They are the most common form of high-level clouds and are found at heights greater than 20,000 feet.

Cirrus clouds are made up of ice crystals from the freezing of supercooled water droplets. Cirrus clouds typically occur in nice weather and point in the direction the air is moving at their elevation. The picture above shows cirrus clouds in the sky.

Fire rainbows are not very common because they occur only under specific conditions. The ice crystals in the cirrus clouds must be hexagonal plates, which means they have six sides and are shaped like a thick plate. Also, the top of these hexagonal plates must be parallel to Earth's surface. Not only that, but the sun must be very high in the sky.

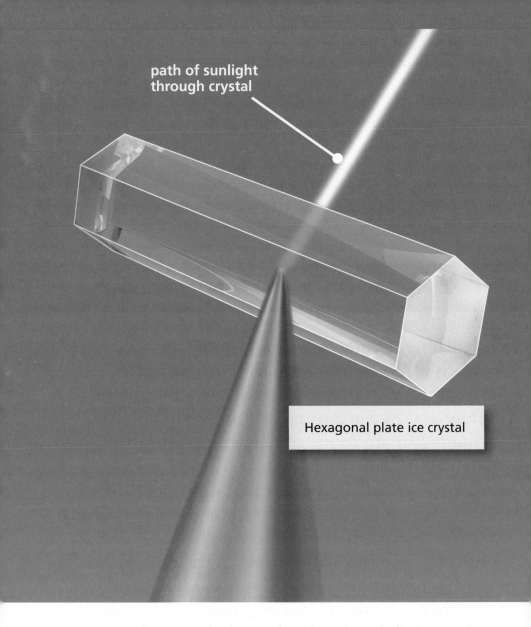

path of sunlight
through crystal

Hexagonal plate ice crystal

How does sunlight make the clouds light up in colors?

Here is a diagram of a hexagonal plate ice crystal. The line shows the path that sunlight travels as it goes through each ice crystal. As the sunlight exits the crystal, its white light is split into the colors of the rainbow. The bending of light through a substance is called **refraction**.

Chapter 2

Raining Cats and Dogs (and Fish)

Have you ever heard the phrase *raining cats and dogs*? No one is really sure where that phrase came from, but some people have guessed it started in 16th century Europe. At that time, poor farmers built their homes with thatched roofs. **Thatch** is a roof covering made of straw or reeds. Often dogs or cats would crawl into the thatch for shelter. Sometimes during a pouring rainstorm, these animals would fall down from the thatch. So the phrase *raining cats and dogs* describes a heavy rainfall.

Although it has never actually rained cats and dogs, there are eyewitness accounts throughout history of people who saw raining animals. The animals most likely to fall from the sky are fish, frogs, and birds, probably because these animals are small and not very heavy.

Cartoon depicting "raining" cats and dogs

How in the world does it rain animals? Powerful updrafts of air during thunderstorms can form mini-tornadoes. A mini-tornado that forms over a river, a lake, or the ocean is called a **waterspout**. A waterspout can pick up water and small fish or frogs that are close to the surface and pull them up into the sky.

Waterspouts can carry the water and animals long distances. When the waterspout touches land, it begins to lose energy, and the water and animals in the spout fall to the ground as rain. The animals often fall to the ground far away from where they were picked up.

A waterspout over the ocean

"Rain of fish" in England on August 6, 2000

A mini-tornado lifted fish out of the sea about a mile offshore.

The tornado carried the fish about a half-mile inland, where they fell on land during a heavy rainstorm.

An "animal rain" occurred in the year 2000 in an English fishing port. After a thunderstorm, small dead fish rained on the town. A retired ambulance driver said, "I thought at first I might have had something wrong with my eyes. The whole of my back yard seemed to be covered in little slivers of silver."

Another example is the yearly rain of fish in Honduras. This event has been happening for more than 100 years. Every year in May or June, a dark storm cloud brings a heavy rainstorm that can last as long as three hours. Afterward, the streets are covered with small fish about six inches long. Most of these fish are alive, so the people pick them up, take them home, and cook them for dinner!

A last example of animal rain is called a bird rain. When a bird rain happens, it's generally the result of a storm overtaking a flock of birds in flight, especially during times of migration. Scientists have observed this in the past with bats as well. Scientists in Texas once witnessed an occurrence on their Doppler weather forecasting equipment where a flock of bats collided with a cyclone!

Chapter 3

Surfing the Amazon River

Imagine waves in a river that are twice as tall as the average man! This can happen during a **tidal bore**—a wave of water that travels up a river against the direction of the current.

The tidal bore on the Amazon River in South America is called the *pororoca*. It forms where the Amazon River flows into the Atlantic Ocean. The word *pororoca* comes from the Tupi language

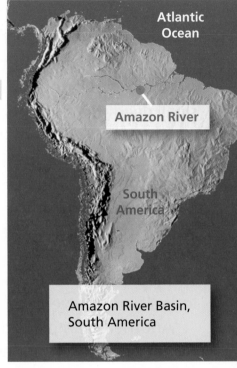

Atlantic Ocean

Amazon River

South America

Amazon River Basin, South America

and means "great destructive noise." The map on this page shows the Amazon River and all the rivers that feed into it. Together these rivers cover more than two million square miles.

The waves of the *pororoca*, which are more than 12 feet high, move at 20 miles per hour. The thunderous roar of the giant waves can be heard from 3 to 6 miles away. People can hear the roar 30 minutes before they see the brown, muddy waves! But this gives them time to prepare for its coming. The waves flood the nearby land and destroy trees, houses, and animals.

What causes this tidal bore?

For most of the year, the Amazon River flows into the Atlantic Ocean for several miles. However, in the dry season, when the water level in the river is low but the ocean tides are very high, the flow reverses, and the ocean flows upstream into the river. The dry season occurs in February and March every year. The conditions are just right for the *pororoca* to push upstream into the river.

Every year, there's a surfing contest to see who can ride the *pororoca* for the longest distance. Riding these waves for miles is thrilling, but it's also very dangerous. Under the muddy waves there might be wreckage from ships, poisonous snakes, alligators, piranhas … and even entire trees! A Brazilian surfer holds the record for surfing the longest distance. In 2003, he rode the wave for 37 minutes and traveled 7.8 miles!

Pororoca on the Amazon River

Not every river in the world has tidal bores. They are very rare and happen in only a few locations worldwide. They only occur where incoming tides

Surfer on a *pororoca*

are funneled into a shallow, narrowing river by way of a broad bay. The funnel-like shape also increases tide height and decreases the amount of time it takes the tide to come in, making the flood appear as a sudden swell. Witnesses to some tidal bores have described them as looking like a wall of water.

Also, the difference between low tide and high tide must be more than 20 feet. In Nova Scotia, Canada, there are tidal bores in the rivers that flow off the Bay of Fundy. The riverbeds often drain completely before a tidal bore occurs. This phenomenon has contributed to claiming the lives of tourists because many enjoy walking into the empty riverbed. Sadly, some get caught in the riverbed when the tidal bore comes, and the "wall of water" drowns them.

The largest tidal bore occurs on the Qiantang River in China. The waves are almost 30 feet high and travel at 25 miles per hour! The Chinese people call it the Silver Dragon. It is so dangerous that nobody who has ever tried to surf it stayed standing for more than 11 seconds, until just a few years ago.

Chapter 4

A Storm That Never Stops

A thunderstorm usually lasts about 20 to 30 minutes. However, in South America, the Catatumbo Lightning thunderstorm seems to be everlasting. It produces lightning for about seven hours every night for 140 to 160 days a year! Sometimes there are 280 flashes every hour. This storm occurs in Venezuela at the mouth of the Catatumbo River where it flows into Lake Maracaibo. The lightning is visible up to 249 miles away.

The electrical discharges in Catatumbo Lightning go between two clouds, rather than between a cloud and the ground. Watching this storm is strange because you can see the lightning, but you can't hear the thunder. The clouds are very high in the sky. Scientists think the thunder is too far away to be heard on the ground.

Catatumbo Lightning

What causes Catatumbo Lightning? No one knows for sure, but scientists think it has to do with methane gas. There is still some debate as to the exact process. Some scientists believe it's related to the landforms in the area. The Andes Mountains are very high above sea level, and Lake Maracaibo is at sea level. The mountains and the lake are very close together. Extremely cold winds blow down from the mountains and collide with the hot, humid air evaporating from the lake. This collision causes the storms and the lightning. Methane gas from the marshes near the lake feeds the storms and keeps the lightning flashing.

Other scientists suggest that a substance called kerogen keeps the lightning flashing. Kerogen is a mixture of organic compounds found in sedimentary rock. Natural gas may leak from these rocks into the marshes and feed the storms.

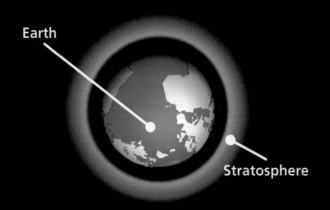

Earth

Stratosphere

Catatumbo Lightning creates large amounts of **ozone**, a gas in Earth's atomosphere. Ozone gas is created when electrical energy is applied to oxygen. In the lower atmosphere, the gas is toxic, but it is quite beneficial when it is in the upper stratosphere. A layer of this gas keeps the sun's harmful rays from reaching Earth.

This ozone layer has been damaged by human activity on Earth, and now more of the sun's harmful rays get through. Some people think that Catatumbo Lightning can help restore the ozone layer. Environmentalist Erik Quiroga says, "This is an exceptional phenomenon, the greatest source of its type, electrical storms, for regenerating the planet's ozone layer."

While there is no way to determine exactly how much ozone is created by the Catatumbo Lightning, it is considered to be the greatest single generator of the gas, judging by the cloud-to-cloud discharge and the frequency of the lightning.

Others would like to capture the power of these storms to provide electricity for homes and businesses.

Chapter 5

Rocks Don't Have Feet, Do They?

How can a rock move across a flat surface by itself? That's exactly what seems to happen on the Racetrack Playa in California. A **playa** is a flat area at the bottom of a desert basin. This satellite photo shows the Racetrack Playa in the mountains of Death Valley National Park.

This 10,000-year-old playa is almost perfectly flat. It is 2.5 miles long and 1.25 miles wide. Its surface is covered with cracked mud made mainly of silt and clay. The playa is very dry, because only a couple of inches of rain fall each year. When it does rain, runoff from the steep mountains around the playa creates a shallow lake on the playa floor.

Racetrack Playa in Panamint Mountains

Racetrack Playa

Rocks of all sizes, loosened by erosion, fall from the mountain slopes onto the playa. Over time, these rocks appear to move with no help from humans or animals. No one has ever seen this phenomenon, but we know they move because we can see the tracks behind them on the playa and because the rocks are often found hundreds of feet from any area they could have fallen from. How in the world can this happen?

Rock with track behind it

Geologists are scientists who study Earth's physical structure. They have determined that these rocks usually move once every two or three years and that their tracks last from three to four years. Rocks with rough bottoms leave straight tracks; rocks with smooth bottoms tend to wander. Sometimes rocks turn over so that a different edge is on the ground, creating a different track.

Geologists have studied the tracks left behind by these rocks. They discovered that some tracks are straight, some tracks zig zag, and others are loops. Sometimes two rock tracks start together, but one of the tracks changes direction. Other times the tracks of two rocks of similar size and shape start together, but one track goes much farther than the other.

Zig zag rock track

Some scientists think that strong wind moves the rocks. After a rainfall, the mud on the surface of the playa becomes wet and very slippery. If a strong wind blows over the playa, it could push the rocks along the wet surface. There is evidence to support this theory, since wind at Racetrack Playa most often blows southwest to northeast and most of the rock trails are parallel to this direction.

Other people think that both wind and ice move the rocks. Some people have reported seeing the playa covered in a layer of ice. The theory is that water freezes around the rocks, embedding the rocks in ice. When strong winds blow, they push the ice sheets across the smooth surface of the playa, and the embedded rocks move with the ice. Some researchers have found trails on the surface of the rocks that they feel support this theory. They believe the trails were caused by ice.

Chapter 6

Giant Crystals

Crystals are everywhere around us—grains of salt and sugar are crystals as are all snowflakes. But these are all tiny crystals. In Mexico, there's a cave with crystals as big as trees!

The Cave of Crystals is 1,000 feet beneath the Naica Mountains of Mexico. No one knew it was there until recently, when workers discovered it while mining lead, zinc, and silver nearby. The mining company wanted to remove water from the mine so that they could dig deeper into the earth. They pumped the water out of the mine, and that removed the water from the cave too.

One day in April 2000, two miners were drilling a new tunnel in the mine. They were surprised to find that it led into a huge cave with giant crystals. The mining company stopped drilling near the cave. They built an iron door at the entrance to keep the crystals safe.

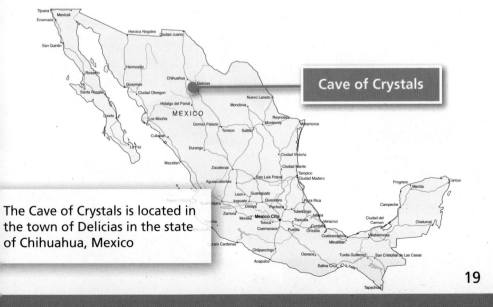

Cave of Crystals

The Cave of Crystals is located in the town of Delicias in the state of Chihuahua, Mexico

The Cave of Crystals is a weird, amazing place. Some of the crystals are as big as trees–4 feet in diameter and 50 feet long. One of these treelike columns can weigh as much as 10 tons. Other crystals look like giant shark teeth piled together. The crystals in this cave are some of the world's largest known natural crystals.

The crystals are composed of selenite, a type of gypsum. Geologists think the crystals grew slowly over thousands of years while the cave was flooded with hot mineral water. They also say that the crystals were able to thrive because the cave had a rare and stable natural environment, which was completely protected from the outside world.

Giant crystals in the Cave of Crystals

The Cave of Crystals is very dangerous for human beings. The temperature is 120° to 136° F, and the humidity is nearly 100 percent. The human body cannot sweat to cool itself, and the brain can't work normally in these conditions. To go into the cave, you must wear an ice-cooled protective suit. Even with a suit, you can stay inside for only a short time.

Penny Boston, a biologist, describes how she felt inside the cave: "Even with the ice-packed suits on, I could feel the strength draining from my arms and legs, and movement growing harder and harder. I felt like I was wading through hot molasses with my brain becoming slower and slower. My temper was unusually short."

As geologists study the cave, they continue to be amazed by it. Geologist Juan Manuel Garcia-Ruiz says "There is no other place on the planet where the mineral world reveals itself in such beauty."

Now Try This

Growing Crystal Spikes

You can grow your own crystals quickly and easily. Find a very warm place, such as a sunny windowsill, for your crystals to grow. It's important for the water to evaporate quickly from the solution, and a sunny place will speed the evaporation. Enjoy!

Materials

dark construction paper
cake pan
clean jar
plastic spoon
¼ cup warm water
1 tablespoon Epsom salt
scissors

1. Find a warm, sunny place to grow your crystals.

2. Use the scissors to cut the construction paper so that it fits into the bottom of the pan.

3. Put the construction paper into the pan.

4. Pour the warm water into the clean jar.

5. Add the Epsom salt to the warm water and stir until the salt is dissolved.

6. Pour the salt solution over the paper in the pan.

7. Put the pan in the warm place. Be careful not to bump or move the pan too much.

8. As the water evaporates, you'll see lots of wonderful spiky crystals!

Glossary

crystal *n.* a solid piece of matter that has a regular arrangement of flat surfaces and angles

fire rainbow *n.* a halo of color in the sky caused by the refraction of sunlight through the ice crystals in cirrus clouds

geologist *n.* someone who studies the Earth's physical structure

ozone *n.* a gas in the Earth's atmosphere

phenomenon *n.* an event that people can perceive through their senses; a remarkable event

playa *n.* a flat area at the bottom of a desert basin

refraction *n.* the bending of light through a substance

thatch *n.* roof covering made of straw or reeds

tidal bore *n.* a wave of water that travels up a river against the direction of the current

waterspout *n.* a mini-tornado that forms over a river, a lake, or the ocean